THE NICE GIRLZ GUIDE TO LIVING
LIFE UNAPOLOGETICALLY

The Emerging Woman

CARMEN RENÈ

The Emerging Woman: The Nice Girlz Guide To Living Life Unapologetically
© 2021 Carmen Renè

Coquí Press
41 Avenida Fernando Luis Ribas
#449
Utuado, Puerto Rico 00641
http://coquipress.com

First edition: September 2021
ISBN: 978-1-7378873-1-7 (Print)
ISBN: 978-1-7378873-0-0 (Ebook)

Cover Illustration: Freepik.com

Notice of Liability
The information in this book is distributed on an "as is" basis, for informational purposes only, without warranty. While every precaution has been taken in the production of this book, neither the copyright owners nor the publisher shall have any liability to any person or entity with respect to any liability, loss, damage caused or alleged to be caused directly or indirectly by the information contained in this book.

Printed in the USA

Table of Contents

Dedication

To my mom, thank you for your strength and all the knowledge that you instilled in me. I would not be the woman I am today if it weren't for your love and support. I love you.

To my son, you have grown into an awesome young man. Keep living your dream. Keep positive energy around you. Continue to elevate and grow. I love you. I am proud of you, and I am your #1 cheerleader.

To my daughters, you are amazing and beautiful. Stay strong and courageous. The world is yours!

To my sisters, you ladies rock! Thank you for always being there for me. I love you all.

To all my friends and family who have supported me, listened to me, and shared things with me. I thank you.

May God Bless each one of you.

Introduction

Who do you think you are with your boldness, your beauty, your sassiness, your self-confidence, your educated self, your movemaking self, your independent self? How dare you walk upright with self-awareness, knowing who you are, whose you are, and what you want out of life! The nerve of you.

Don't we all want to be everything I just mentioned? Wouldn't it be absolutely amazing if you actually felt what I like to call your "Sha Na Na" in your soul and your spirit, everything that people felt you had the nerve to be?

What if I told you that you are very capable of being all those things and more? However, it will require some work on your end. That "work" is called giving yourself permission to live unapologetically, giving the world exactly who you were created to be. And the work and the journey looks different for each individual.

To the strong but quiet introverted woman who is at that pivotal moment in her life where she wants to break through her shell and no longer hide her true identity for the benefit of others...

To the smart career woman who has been passed over for promotion because her coworkers are threatened by her education and experience...

To the entrepreneur who wants to scale her business and become a profitable organization, but is reluctant to bring her ideas to the table because of fear of rejection from others...

To the woman who suffers from social engagement/anxiety, but seeks approval from her peers...

To the creative woman who wants to be comfortable with her thoughts, her energy, her talents...

To all women who are looking to evolve into who you were created to be, who want to be happy living authentically, unapologetically, and according to her own terms, this book is for you. You were not meant to fit in a box. We were not created to be the same. Wouldn't that be boring? Allow your creativity, your boldness, your sassiness and your true colors shine. The world is waiting on you to EMERGE.

8 Questions
to Think About

What Really Makes You Tick? On your quest with the desire to connect with yourself, before you read the chapters in this book, think about the following questions:

Who are you?

Today's generation has endeavored to redefine the 'self,' or at least that is what it appears to be. So how do you describe yourself?

What type of life do you want?

This is a question that is asked quite often. Today, social media tells us who we should be and what type of life we should have. An example would be living like an entertainer (artist, actress, dancer, etc). We are not aware of what an entertainer is presenting on social media if is true or false. So what type of life do you picture for yourself?

What do you value?

Have morals, standards, integrity, honesty, and respect gone bye-bye? What boundaries have you created for yourself?

Are you comfortable in your own skin?

Do you honor and love what you represent?

To receive honor and respect you must first give it to yourself.

In your everyday life, (work, social life, relationships, partnerships, etc.) Are you happy or do you appear to be happy?

You can be just about anything you always wanted to be, but to realize that presenting a false impression of something you're not can become exhausting.

What does emerging into living life authentically and unapologetically mean to you?

**What makes you tick?
What inspires you overall?**

Chapter One

What Does "The Emerging Woman" Mean?

Giving the universe
the gift of you.

Sometimes, you may wonder if some people are born fabulous, awesome, strong, confident, bold, or amazing. Well, they aren't. Having those qualities or characteristics is a choice. Having self-esteem and learning self-identification is a choice; it is not a talent. It is the power of your decision to set the tone for who you want to be and how you want to live. You do not need permission to do the things that I mentioned. Blows your mind, right?

I get it. It is challenging to develop your true identity when there are things like social media telling you who you should be and how you should live. Social media can brainwash you and manipulate your subconscious on who you think you should be, to the point where it almost feels like you're in a battle with yourself and social media. Well, let's strap on the right armor and fight for who you were created to be. And please be aware that you will get knocked down and beat up, but that's okay. The fight is worth it!

Do you have the same challenge on the job, in your business, with family, friends, and spouses? Yes? All of us do. Our bosses, business partners, children, significant others all want us to show up in a manner that is fulfilling to them. And we do it. Why? Because as women, we have not learned the power of saying NO! Am I right? No need to be ashamed, I was guilty of the same thing. I was guilty of "just doing" something because I was asked or I was needed. I was guilty of not speaking my mind. I was guilty of being too nice. I was guilty of not putting my foot down and not setting boundaries. I was guilty of showing up even when I didn't want to. I was guilty of appearing to be happy when I really wasn't. I was faking it more often than I would like to admit.

Does this sound familiar? Let me be clear, there is nothing wrong with some of those things, like being nice, passionate, and wanting everyone to be happy. The problem develops when you lose who you are to make others happy and always meeting and exceeding the expectations of others while burying your own. You forgot about you, my friend. I once forgot about me too. The resolution to these challenges for me was learning how to create boundaries and not deviate from them. I had to work on managing my emotions, determining what type of life I wanted to live, and living that life authentically and unapologetically. I had to transform into a new woman who now sets the tone for how she wants to be treated and live her life based on who she was created to be. The "Emerging Woman" simply means that you no longer march to the beat of someone else's drum, and you've learned to create your own. It means that you have evolved into being the woman that you were created to be.

No more 'Ms. Nice Girl' - She has exited the building.

Living authentically and unapologetically will eventually lead to overall self-improvement when you start becoming responsible for who you are, what you have, and what you do. It is a flame that spreads like a brush fire from the inside out. When you develop self-identification, you take control of how you present and how you represent yourself.

Self-identification brings about self-improvement, true assessment, and determination. So how do you start creating the building blocks of self-identification? Keep reading and I will share my journey, with the hope that you are inspired to start or continue yours.

Reflections

*You do not need anyone's
permission to live
unapologetically.*

*You have accepted certain
unfulfilling behaviors over the years,
and it is okay.*

*To live in your true authenticity,
you must look inward and self-identify
with who you are.*

Reflections

Enter your own personal reflections here.

Thought Exercise

Apply what you just read to your unique
life and experiences.

✳ *Where in your life do you need to give yourself
permission to be authentic?*

_____

_____

_____

_____

✳ *Who have you allowed to take advantage of your
kindness?*

_____

_____

_____

_____

✳ *What tools or resources do you need to learn
self-improvement?*

_____

_____

_____

_____

Chapter Two

The Emerging Woman Who? Me?

What you give to the world should not be faked or forced!

"**G**irl, you better shut your mouth! Suck it up and keep it moving. There's no crying in Corporate America." That is what I told myself as I entered the dreadful walls of yet another day at my corporate job. Some days I would just sit at my desk and think to myself, "Why am I even here? I am not valued. I am ignored. My work is not recognized, and it is clear that some of my coworkers and managers do not like me and/or do not feel I deserve to be in the same room because of my skin color. Why am I even putting in the effort? I show up, perform to what I think is the highest level of excellence, speak the corporate language, laugh at corny jokes, dress "the right way," and play the nice, well-mannered and behaved Black girl. Why can't I just be me? Oh my gosh, it is exhausting, it doesn't feel right, and I don't like it. So, what do I do? I still need a paycheck, right?"

I assume that you have had similar feelings. You may not have or have had these same emotions, but I am sure you could apply it to many aspects of your life. Whether it is in a business you own and operate, personal and/or business relationships, or in your religion's practices, I am 99% sure that you have, consciously or unconsciously uttered the words "If only I could just be myself." I am here to tell you that you are not alone. Our universe has over eight billion human beings, yet many of us are walking around like fictitious characters, being someone we're not. Hell! Where is the **authenticity** in that?

> We will explore the meaning of **authenticity** in the next chapter.

I have stated those exact words repeatedly. But I still seem to normalize how people think I should operate. It was only when I started to accept who I am in my natural skin and put my foot down that I was able to control how I showed up. I no longer give that power to anyone else to tell me who I am, how I should talk, how I should act or react, or how I should look. I own that!

If you are thinking, well Carmen, how did you get to be bold enough to own how you show up to the world? Well, I'm glad you asked. I want you to think about the word "IDENTITY". Like most adults, especially women, we have no clue who we are. We know that we wake up, do our morning, afternoon, and evening routine, and we go back to bed and Lord willing, we get back up and repeat the same thing the next day.

We know that we are wives, mothers, grandmothers, career women, entrepreneurs, friends, sisters, and daughters. But we have no clue about the private, deeply revealing inner workings of our mind, body, and soul. We just walk around like little robots. So, I decided to start having conversations with myself about who I am, what I genuinely want, and what type of life I wanted to live. I started being honest with myself about who I was without the makeup, perfume, jewelry and designer clothing.

I have learned that I am a multi-dimensional human being. I am like an onion made up of multiple layers. For example, I am a very friendly person, but I am also an introvert. I am very diplomatic. My most fulfilling life direction is to see the world and learn everything

I can from it. What this means is that I must insert myself in an environment so I can do and be all the things that I just mentioned. We have so many distractions, and so many things that tell us who we should be. Social Media has a huge impact and influence on how we should be and live our lives.

I am a firm believer that if you allow someone to determine who you are, your life will be unfulfilled and inconsistent because you will never have the opportunity to become who you were created to be. The solution is to focus on who you are; direct your attention away from the status quo and social norms. The goal is to determine who you are and your unique traits, but how can you do this when you do not know who you are to begin with? The chapter reflections and thought exercise after each chapter will help guide you through the process of identifying who you are. The journey must start somewhere, my beautiful, smart, intelligent ladies. Why not start now?

Reflections

*Understand who you are
and why you were created.
TIP: Do not compare yourself
to anyone else. You are how
you are supposed to be in
your own naked skin.*

*This is your personal journey
of self-identification; accept
the essence of who you are.*

Reflections

Enter your own personal reflections here.

I believe the most successful people in the universe are people who have mastered the "art" of just being themselves

You get to decide how you want to show up!

Now that you have learned that it is okay to show up as yourself, you might be thinking, "Who Am I?". Seems quite funny to be asking yourself this question at this point in your life, right? As little girls we dreamt of being a movie star, a singer, a doctor, a teacher, a wife, or a mother. But as grown women, we tend to draw a blank and our hearts begin to palpitate when we're asked those three words, "Who Are You?". What are you afraid of? Are you afraid that you won't like who you are? If you really dig deep in your heart and soul, would you see a stranger, someone that you don't even recognize or couldn't identify?

Breathe.

I know those words might have punched you in the pit of your stomach, and that's okay. Here is what I know for sure: until you start having the conversation with yourself about who you truly are, and what you genuinely want, you will always be bothered. But the beauty in this is that you get to decide how you want to show up. Take a second to honor the fact that you get to decide who you want to be.

The best version of yourself is being true to yourself, but what does this mean? Your perspective determines the outcome that you see and experience, as well as what you see for yourself in terms of self-worth. If you so desire to understand *you*, you must be clear about what that looks like. You are human, so don't get frustrated if it takes what seems like a lifetime to understand who you are and what you represent. Honor that you have the audacity to want to live life based on who you were created to be and have the experiences you want.

Sometimes it's easier to explain something by identifying what it's not. That said, here is a list of what is not being the best version of yourself:

1. Being true to yourself is *not* about pleasing others.

2. Being true to yourself is *not* about hurting others.

3. Being true to yourself is *not* about doing things you dislike.

4. Being true to yourself is *not* about forcing yourself to do something.

5. Being true to yourself is *not* about being hard on yourself.

6. Being true to yourself is *not* about judging others and comparing yourself.

7. Being true to yourself is *not* about being a victim of your surroundings.

8. Being true to yourself is *not* about acting in a way that will attract more fans on social media.

Bonus
IDENTITY QUIZ

The following questions will help you identify which area of your life that's the best version of yourself. Whether the answer is yes or no, pick the option that's closest to how you feel. Then, circle the responses you answered most in each category (mostly yes or mostly no).

BUSINESS, CAREER AND PROFESSIONAL WORLD

	YES	NO
Are you satisfied with your work?	☐	☐
Do you get along with your colleagues?	☐	☐
Do you know what you want to do for work?	☐	☐
Are you comfortable with your knowledge and skills?	☐	☐
Do you feel you are contributing to the world in a way that fulfills you?	☐	☐
Are you happy in your career?	☐	☐
Given the opportunity to change work, would you still stay in your job/career?	☐	☐
	YES	NO
TOTAL		

LOVE AND ROMANTIC RELATIONSHIPS

	YES	NO
■ Are you experiencing happiness in love?	☐	☐
■ Do you feel like you can be yourself in a love relationship?	☐	☐
■ Do you feel your partner knows you very well?	☐	☐
■ Are your needs being met in your love relationship?	☐	☐
■ Is it easy for you to understand your partner?	☐	☐
■ Are you healthily independent in your love relationship?	☐	☐

	YES	NO
TOTAL		

You are no longer shrinking yourself to be digestible... You can choke!

*T*here is power and strength in working on and learning about yourself. Sounds like an easy thing to do, right? Through my own journey, I found it to be quite challenging, primarily because I didn't want to look at myself in the mirror and try to discover who I genuinely was. And better yet, I didn't want to accept how long I had gone through life showing up as someone I wasn't. But at some point, I knew I had to look at my life and my character and be honest with myself and ask some difficult questions.

Why am I so caught up in what others think about how I should live and operate in my life? How long am I going to continue to wear this mask that I have worn for years? Who was I created to be? Why do I feel it is my mission to be free and encourage others to do the same? Who do I think I am? I wanted to self reflect and develop the ability to shift my mindset to live a more authentic life; a life where I'm in the driver seat. I understood that with this shift in mindset, there were some habits or principles that I had to live by daily. I will share them with you.

• • • • • Principle 1 • • • • •

I prayed. I prayed and asked God to reveal my purpose, why I was created in this lifetime, His mission for me, and I prayed that my ears would be sensitive enough to hear His Words.

• • • • • Principle 2 • • • • •

I accepted who I was and forgave myself for trying to be someone I was not. I stopped being so hard on myself and learned to laugh at the silly mistakes or lessons I had learned along the way. I knew there was certainly a point in time where I wasn't true to myself. Oftentimes when I altered things about myself to work at a certain job, for example, or entertained a certain type of relationship, none of these things felt good. But I have accepted that that was only a season in my life, and that season did not define me. I stand in my truth now and have embraced the person I used to be, because that person has molded me into the person I am today.

· · · · · Principle 3 · · · · ·

I refrained from looking for acknowledgement and acceptance from others. Sure, accolades like "job well done," and being told that you're awesome feel great. But I realized that more often than not, I was my own cheerleader. I had to give myself permission to pat myself on the back. And that's okay. I no longer wait to be validated or appreciated by another human being. If it happens, great! If it doesn't, it's still great. I have learned to love and accept me. If I do not love myself first, who will?

· · · · · Principle 4 · · · · ·

I increased my standards and boundaries. Setting limits is one of many important steps that I had to master before I could emerge into living life authentically. I realized that if I allowed anyone to set the tone for my life, I wasn't living in my true identity. Who knows me better than me, right? Leaving my life in the hands of others would never have allowed me to truly live and be free.

· · · · ·  Principle 5 · · · · ·

I freed myself from the opinions of people. And this was no disrespect to anyone, and it was certainly not about my ego. The truth was I would never be able to live up to anyone's opinion of me—favorable or unfavorable. In truth, I no longer have the desire to do so. For those who feel it's their place to judge, I say have your opinions. I am very adamant about letting people know that their opinions are fine, but their disrespect will not be accepted or tolerated!

· · · · ·  Principle 6 · · · · ·

I released anything to its destiny that did not align with my growth. Things that were not aligned to the experiences I wanted to have in life I purged. Anyone who wasn't helping me grow and be a better person, I had to distance myself from them. I learned in doing this that sometimes I had to stand alone, but at least I was standing with someone who had my best interest at hand: me.

Living by and adapting to these principles have created a happier space in my life. It is a happier space because I choose to stand in my power and be respected rather than be liked. I am a true believer that energy can jump from person to person. I no longer allow anyone access to my space who does not match my energy. Some of my acquaintances, family, and friends had a difficult time accepting my new approach or rules. Even the leadership at my place of employment started giving me the side eye. But I was still employed.

My new attitude, if you will, is simple: you can accept me or not. And I must say, having such an attitude is very liberating. But I was only able to adopt this type of thinking when I decided to ask myself those hard questions, forgave myself for not having the wisdom that I have today, and accepted who I was and who I wasn't. So now, I can show up strong and bold in the workplace, in business, in my relationships and friendships. And I have God to thank for showing me the way.

Reflections

*Your journey in discovering
you may be challenging,
but that's okay.*

*Create principles or affirmations
to help guide you through your
journey of self-discovery.*

Believe in and bet on you.

Reflections

Enter your own personal reflections here.

Thought Exercise

Apply what you just read to your unique
life and experiences.

✳ *Have you asked yourself those hard questions about
your purpose and mission? If so, what did you
discover?*

_____

_____

_____

_____

✳ *What principles can you live by that will help you to
stand in your power?*

_____

_____

_____

_____

✳ *Who or what do you need to purge in your life that will
allow you to live in your authenticity?*

_____

_____

_____

_____

Chapter
Five

The Change

. . . .

They are not going to like you.

Once I started doing the work on myself, I was able to accept who God created me to be. What I learned along this journey and also accepted was that everyone is not going to like the *new* me, and that they preferred the old version of me. Allow me to explain.

Note: To protect the identity of those involved, names and identifiable information won't be shared or have been altered.

I was in a relationship for several years. In my relationship, my partner had gotten comfortable with me being passive, quiet, chronically forgiving, kind, and nice. This was his mindset until the day I totally lost it. I let him have it. He was every name that I'm for certain is not written in the Bible.

His fault, right? He was warned many times. You see, at this point I had already begun to do the work on me, but of course my partner was not familiar with this "new" person and did not know how to treat her. Because of vows, beliefs, wanting to work it out, blah blah blah, the relationship went on longer than it should have, and in that moment the best thing that I could do, so that I didn't end up in jail, was focus on me and my wellbeing.

Here is the beautiful thing. That relationship taught me so many life lessons. Lessons are meant to make you better. I am better at controlling my emotions. Can I tell you the beauty in being able to manage my emotions? I am better at being honest and up front about my wants, needs, desires, and the requirements to have my full attention. I have learned to set standards and boundaries early on in a relationship and not deviated from them. I have learned that even in a partnership/marriage I still can decide and set expectations and not feel guilty about it.

In that relationship I also picked up what some would call negative traits. I was already a "one and done" type of person, for the most part. Today, a guy doesn't stand a chance. As my granny would always say, "You bet not," not you better not, but you bet not. So, for the guys, you bet not look, sniff, sneeze, cough, blink, or breathe the wrong way or you are cancelled, done, finito. It is "Bye Fernando" for me.

Of course, I'm being silly, but the truth is, this is one of many examples where me changing for the better made some folks uncomfortable. So, I am saying to you, friend! Be Brave! Be Strong! As you begin the journey of being the new you, you will find out that the impossible has just become a bit more possible.

Surround yourself with people who like or love you for who you truly are. Take time to nurture the relationships that inspire you to be the best version of yourself and learn to create healthy boundaries in relationships that bring you down. You have control over who you develop a relationship with or not. That is how you will step into your power by respecting yourself and allow healthy relationships to develop and grow.

Your inner voice is probably one of the most important types of communication and, by far, the most influential. Use that as a tool to guide you through your relationships.

Chapter
Six

Increase Your Self Awareness!

. . . .

Getting deeper
with your inner self

Let's talk about self-awareness. You may ask "what is being aware of self and why is it so important"? Being self-aware is looking at you, my dear. Your DNA both inside and out. You may not like what you discover about yourself, but you get to decide what that looks like. And I will help you, which is another bonus! Below are my top six reasons on why self-awareness is important to me, and I ask that you look deeply and see if you can find yourself there:

Self-awareness is the ability to recognize your emotional state and find ways to stay in balance. When you practice self-awareness, you are automatically allowing yourself to be a better version of yourself and not let your emotions take control of you.

Being self-aware simply means that you can observe yourself from a non-judgmental perspective. When you are self-aware, you can catch yourself in the present moment experiencing a specific state, reaction, or feeling. The more you are aware of your emotions and behaviors, the more you start to understand yourself.

The ultimate reward to being self-aware is your ability to recognize when you are not in alignment with your true self. It is the opportunity to be authentic and therefore have integrity in yourself. Self-awareness is the key to becoming the best version of yourself. Self-awareness will help you in your daily life with identifying moments when you are not yourself, where you react from a place of fear or anger. When you become aware of that, it becomes easier to realign with the best version of yourself.

You will experience a greater ability to recognize your emotions. Self-awareness means that you can observe yourself and your emotions. Instead of being reactive or dramatic, you can take notice and acknowledge that some situations have triggered an emotional reaction. It will help you prevent actions or words that are often said or done in the heat of emotions.

You will improve your critical thinking. The more you practice self-awareness, the more you can provide positive feedback to yourself. That way, you do not behave with a fake identity or act out your life.

Your relationships will improve. I promise (smiley face). Self-awareness can help improve relationships because you stop trying to please the other person and intuitively align yourself with who you truly are. Showing a side of you that is authentic and genuine.

Self-awareness is observing yourself in real-time, encouraging mindfulness. When you are self-aware, you can immediately acknowledge when you are experiencing something that doesn't feel good or right. Within a moment, you can shift what you are doing to something more pleasing, more fun. By observing yourself, you will become more conscious of the things you enjoy doing and what you do not like. It will become your compass to happiness.

Reflections

*Self-awareness helps
to align your mind,
body, and spirit.*

*Your entire life will improve
by increasing your
self-awareness*

Reflections

Enter your own personal reflections here.

Thought Exercise

Apply what you just read to your unique
life and experiences.

✳ *List the areas of your life that are most in alignment.*

_____

_____

_____

_____

_____

_____

✳ *List the areas of your life where you need alignment.*

_____

_____

_____

_____

_____

_____

_____

Chapter Seven

Connecting with Your Authenticity

Character traits
of an authentic person.

*T*o connect with your authenticity, you must understand the character traits of an authentic individual. How do I know? Because connecting to my authenticity was a process in my individual journey.

I first looked up the definition of authentic. Authentic is defined as: "Not false or copied; genuine; real." And, my favorite definition, "representing one's true nature or beliefs; true to oneself or to the person identified."

Once I understood the definition I did a self-check, of my lifestyle and identified specific areas where I was not living as my "True Self". Here are a few things that I discovered about myself, which was an indication that I was not aligned with my true self:

At Work

- I was not satisfied with my employment or professional life.

- I was not comfortable with my abilities and felt the constant need to reinvent my skills.

- I felt that I was not contributing in a fulfilling way.

In Relationships

- I was unhappy in my relationships.

- I am a giver, so I was over functioning and forgot to take care of me.

- My needs weren't being met in many relationships (platonic, work and romantic).

Socially

- I am 70 percent introverted. I was sometimes uncomfortable in my own skin.

- Entertaining is sometimes uncomfortable, but I do it anyway.

- I can talk myself out of dining out just because it takes so much energy to be comfortable around others. I am sure my fellow introverts can relate.

In discovering these things about myself, I learned that being true means that I behave and communicate in complete integrity with my beliefs, values, and, most of all, with what feels right in my heart. I am proof that when there is alignment with your inner self (emotional state and desires) and outer self (behaviors and communication), you are the best version of yourself. Sounds fantastic, right?

Reflections

*Discovering things
about yourself that you
were not previously aware
of is intriguing.*

Self-checks are a must.

Reflections

Enter your own personal reflections here.

Thought Exercise

Apply what you just read to your unique
life and experiences.

✳ *Do you believe that you are living an authentic life on
your terms? Explain.*

_____

_____

_____

_____

_____

_____

✳ *List characteristics about yourself that you love.*

_____

_____

_____

_____

_____

_____

Chapter Eight

Live Life Unapologetically

. . . .

Enjoy the experience.

I hope that you have learned that, from the time you were born, you may have been forced to be a version of yourself that pleases others. Whether it comes from the way you were raised or how you were taught in school, you may have learned to put on a mask and be an actor in your life.

I hope that you understand that we all know someone who seems to be genuine and authentic and lives an incredibly happy life. It is sometimes difficult to comprehend what they did to get there. So, if you did not know anyone prior to reading this book, who is very intentional about being genuine and authentic, you now know me! Yay! I have shared with you some of my personal experiences and habits that I developed on how I got to living life unapologetically.

Here is the last bonus. Remember this:

Authentic people are genuine, real, and mostly operating with integrity within themselves. They don't try to be someone they are not or please people they don't know or whose opinion shouldn't matter. They, in some way, know that they are unique, but accept that aspect of themselves. For them, being different isn't an issue or something they strive to be; they are just themselves.

Authentic people also love doing what they enjoy and don't try to copy others' ideas for the sake of being happy and/or successful. Their success and happiness come from doing what's in their heart and what drives them, as opposed to what inspires others. When you do the things that you love, you are being authentic, you are exposing the best version of yourself, and that is why it is fulfilling.

Another way to reconnect with your true and authentic self is to rediscover your inner child, the one that didn't care about what others thought. Try to be more like your inner child and awaken that aspect of you that you knew when you were young, but somehow disconnected from once you grew up. Take the time to play again, to make mistakes, forgive and try something else. Don't be afraid to be vulnerable and do what your heart tells you to do, no matter what others may think. And most of all, learn to live in the present moment.

Reflections

Enter your own personal reflections here.

Thought Exercise

Apply what you just read to your unique
life and experiences.

✳ *How will you live life on your own terms?*

_____

_____

_____

_____

_____

_____

✳ *Will you live life unapologetically and EMERGE? Explain.*

_____

_____

_____

_____

_____

_____

_____

CPSIA information can be obtained
at www.ICGtesting.com
Printed in the USA
LVHW010459290921
698991LV00008B/566